A So[illegible]nar

A Sonogrammar

Kay L Are

Puncher & Wattmann

First published in 2025
Published by Puncher & Wattmann
PO Box 279
Waratah NSW 2298

info@puncherandwattmann.com

NATIONAL LIBRARY OF AUSTRALIA

A catalogue record for this book is available from The National Library of Australia.

ISBN 9781923099432

Cover design by Kay L Are

Printed by Lightning Source International

Contents

V Algorhythms II

Sorties

Glazed glitter.
A red stamp.
Mildred's umbrella.
Objects.
Water raining.
Peeled pencil, choke.
A substance in a cushion.
A dog.
It was black, black took.
A long dress.
A time to eat.
A feather.
A petticoat.

Symploce tic

supposing you do not like to change
anything suitable is so necessary
absurd is actual is all that it showed
nothing strange
there was a time certainly
it, mixed with/without a blaming
so clean is a light
is there any extreme use
a little called anything is a little called
a shallow hole

Objective correlatives

VI Window pictures (still life)

VII Hew

Notes, acknowledgements, references

Parataxidermy (still life)

it was during that summer that she first felt a desire to
express the rhythm of the visible world.

Gertrude Stein, *The Autobiography of Alice B. Toklas*

OBJECTS

GLAZED GLITTER.

Nickel, what is nickel, it is originally rid of a cover.

The change in that is that red weakens an hour. The change has come. There is no search. But there is, there is that hope and that interpretation and sometime, surely any is unwelcome, sometime there is breath and there will be a sinecure and charming very charming is that clean and cleansing. Certainly glittering is handsome and convincing.

There is no gratitude in mercy and in medicine. There can be breakages in Japanese. That is no programme. That is no color chosen. It was chosen yesterday, that showed spitting and perhaps washing and polishing. It certainly showed no obligation and perhaps if borrowing is not natural there is some use in giving.

A RED HAT.

A dark grey, a very dark grey, a quite dark grey is monstrous ordinarily, it is so monstrous because there is no red in it. If red is in everything it is not necessary. Is that not an argument for any use of it and even so is there any place that is better, is there any place that has so much stretched out.

A BLUE COAT.

A blue coat is guided guided away, guided and guided away, that is the particular color that is used for that length and not any width not even more than a shadow.

A PIANO.

If the speed is open, if the color is careless, if the selection of a strong scent is not awkward, if the button holder is held by all the waving color and there is no color, not any color. If there is no dirt in a pin and there can be none scarcely, if there is not then the place is the same as up standing.

This is no dark custom and it even is not acted in any such a way that a restraint is not spread. That is spread, it shuts and it lifts and awkwardly not awkwardly the centre is in standing.

son that there is more snips are the same shining very colored rid of no round color.

A NEW CUP AND SAUCER.

Enthusiastically hurting a clouded yellow bud and saucer, enthusiastically so is the bite in the ribbon.

OBJECTS.

Within, within the cut and slender joint alone, with sudden equals and no more than three, two in the centre make two one side.

If the elbow is long and it is filled so then the best example is all together.

The kind of show is made by squeezing.

EYE GLASSES.

A color in shaving, a saloon is well placed in the centre of an alley.

A CUTLET.

A blind agitation is manly and uttermost.

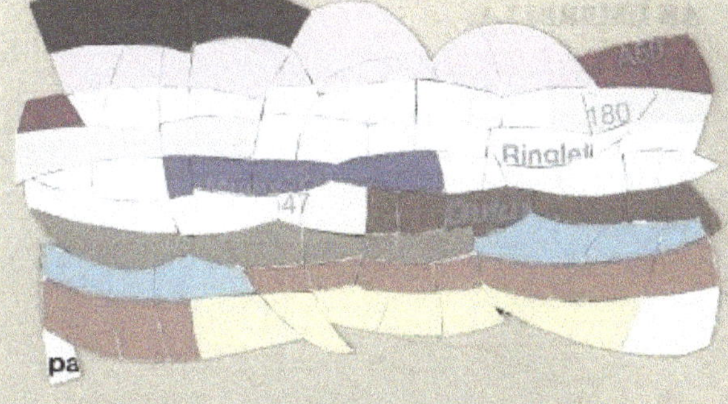

RED ROSES.

A cool red rose and a pink cut pink, a collapse and a sold hole, a little less hot.

COLORED HATS.

Colored hats are necessary to show that curls are worn by an addition of blank spaces, this makes the difference between single lines and broad stomachs, the least thing is lightening, the least thing means a little flower and a big delay a big delay that makes more nurses than little women really little women. So clean is a light that nearly all of it shows pearls and little ways. A large hat is tall and me and all custard whole.

A FEATHER.

A feather is trimmed, it is trimmed by the light and the bug and the post, it is trimmed by little leaning and by all sorts of mounted reserves and loud volumes. It is surely cohesive.

A BROWN.

A brown which is not liquid not more so is relaxed and yet there is a change, a news is pressing.

Algorhythms I

Conjunctions

An object is not an object; it is a witness to a relationship.

Cecilia Vicuña

a bow is every color very colored

and makes all the waving
color the particular color that is used
for that length, coloring a colored sky
a sky-colored grey – a sick color

that is grey-rose wood, a not-torn-rose
wood color lead in color, a color in shaving a dinner
set of colored china
and more of the same color
than could have been expected

of a single hurt color and a color that is
no color chosen and certainly discolor,
a particular color strangely rid
of no round color, not straw color and
not coal color – never more coal color, a color darker
sooner than a choice
in color – the change of color is
likely an established color

and cunning: there is no color,
not any color, no color not any color

if red is in everything

if the red is rose – if the button
holder is held
        by all the waving
        color and there
        is no
        color
if the color
        is careless if it is
        white and black
if the speed is open
if the elbow is long and it is
        filled if lilies are
        lily white if
        it is brighter if inside is
        let in
if the selection of a strong scent
        is not awkward if borrowing
        is not natural
if it is
there places change
if they do this
        and   they do this
                if the party is small if you suppose this
                in August
                if there is a genuine interest in there
                being present
                as many girls as men
they dusty
will dirt a surface if they exhaust
noise and distance and even
dust if dust is
        washed off

            if it is
            not necessary
                        if there is no pleasure in not
                        getting tired of it
            and there is
            if there is
            no more spreading
if   there
            is no more spreading
if there is if
there   is not

foliage and grace and a new

cup and saucer, a laugh and a
lip and a laid climb, sudden
and at the same time
patient and staring and
too late
and later
all this and not ordinary
noise and distance and even dust
spitting and perhaps washing
and polishing
the lamp and the cake and a sweet
singing trimming by length and
by doubling in the stem and
in starting
it shuts
            and it lifts
                        the six and the seven, a glass
and a cousin, the bug and the
post, nearer
and farther a meadow and
a stroke, a lining and the shape, the cut
and slender joint
and soap and silk for
cleaning, scatter and scattering
concentrating the illusion
and the illustration, astonishing
and difficult in mercy
and in medicine
readiness and eyesight are guided
and guided away
            a whole sight and a little
groan and sometime
a collapse and a sold hole, old

ladies and mild colds
three and more and no more
        than three
and clean and cleansing
a sweetness and some of that
habitual and tyrannical and authorised and educated and
resumed and articulate and sometime
next best nearest a pillar
        a cause and no curve
and a hat and hurt
and courage and a clock
and matches and a swan:
        a red thing and a white thing, noon
and moon
leadish and nearly
set in

what is a spectacle

what is it what was
the use
what is
the wind

what is the sash
like
            is the bite in the ribbon
a realistic
what

is the current that makes
machinery what
is this current
what was
the use
of a whole time of a violent kind
of delightfulness

what is lead what is nickel does it whow
does it not whow whow
is it
            likely
does this
change
is it
disappointing
is it
not necessary
that a change
and how
            soon

act so that there is no use in a center

it is not very likely that there is a center, a hill is a
hill and no hill is contained in a pink tender descender.

Gertrude Stein, 'Rooms'

the center is
not well placed
in the center

yet two in
the center
make two
one side

spread into nothing: a fugue

bend more. gather more as it is.
cooling, collect more   trembling,
cut more than is. actual and more,

more places not empty in any kind
of place. is there any place
that has so much. stretched out

there is no more. to do about it

more than the more certain
and more likely the more. reason, a sign
of more in let in. to replace
any substance
and there. places change

a dark place is not a dark
place   is there any place. that is better

hardly more than much more
joy even more melodiously, even more
hurt than more being

together more. no more handling
is needed
like anything mustard.
cause a whole thing to be strange
in everything if red is in
everything and just. so much more
is there. more than not even more
than a shadow. more of the same. then

the place is the same as roundness,
more water is broken
in more places easily. much more. easily
is practiced and a place
to put them not misplaced,
no more spreading change
in. and even more is enough

for that. if there is MORE and nothing
else, nothing quite flat, the kind
of. thing spread
into nothing. anything
shows. shudders. makes lying places
in between. a place, places and a revision
directly placed back. not more in front

not more in front. mention nothing
and no. more does more to choosing,
shows more mounting than anything
between, curves. more
particularly it addresses no more

the least thing – the not empty
circular side place – a place in. more places.

more nurses than little women
broken. in more places. in the center
and mended best to show sudden

places. the little things, the place between
the half. no use for any more. places
to accustom the thing. best thing, something
very like the last. time
well placed that, hardening more,
sighs last

all prepositions of place performed in order

a cus [giving [japan [medicine [mer [a system [gl [Kind in] ass in] change in] cy in] breakages in] ese in] substance in] hion

behind

what will be [feather and [appe [a change in] arance in] cotton in] a table

not [No pleasure in] getting

before

sew [care [the bed in] less
ness in] ing }out

out of} the way out of} kindness out of} rudeness out of} an eye out of

any [a whole [refusing [any kind [there is a quotation in] of place in] to believe in] piece in] case

under

morning light enough [stand [a blight quite [not men [no new [selection in] table in] tioned in] solid in] ing in] if inside is let in

on

the table

on

the table

on

gre [buy [summer [singular
[the table in] arrangement in]
and winter in] ing in] en

by

if [suppose no [summer and [the
necessary [August [even [start [the
[whi [whi [a mark in] te in] te in]
stem in] ing in] ing in] even in]
incident in] winter] red in] red is in

showing that [a wise [stand [any such [a [out in] pin in] way in] ing in] veil in] there is

resemblance

the [the darkness [the circular / between / side place in] and right in] way

more [more [the center of [shav [the cen
[the [the rib [several kinds [besides in] of oceans in] bon within] cut in]
ter in] ing in] an alley in] in] places in]

the water
the deci [no [yell [half between in] ow in] size in] sion

in front
behind
in front

there [ord [the [wood hold in] rush in] er in] having

into nothing into

single old curves and a nothing

pen between nies

place
out between lines
lad between ies

on
where there is [the top in] a tight head

fairy sea [nearer in] nearer and
sigh [farther in] t
{cough out
the lea [cough out in] ther

wh [sit in] en
on
red

the [and [a shallow hole in] in] middle of

(a)
rubbed [rubbed [si [a sold [a ga (tiny) te in] gn in] ier in] purr in] purr
(spot)
(within)

strange [get nearest a pillar in] steps beside rest nearest
a pillar

ja [jack in] ck

if one is on the table one is the same length

that is one
way to breed

and a custom which is
necessary if
(two one side) one uses
one way
not to shatter

all the numbers in Rooms

there is none there empty.
none. none at all.
a preparation is given to the ones
preparing to do it one way. A little sign
of an entrance is the one
that made it a plain hill, one is
not that.
between one window and another
one taste one tack, one taste
one bottle, one taste one fish,
one taste one barometer for another one
and another one, each one
so stationary that there are invitations. this does not
seem strange to one. is one more naughty
in a spectacle   the whole section is one season, every room
is open, there were two
together. comparing these two comes to be
two of whom are not separating – any two
were indifferent and yet they were all connecting
the two tables in all the time.
there are three days when there are not four
surely there were four – four are no more
than were taller.
suppose that any five suppose
that the five are all the wonder
of six little spoons
– tender and true all along the tendency
in a pink
tender descender –
this is fifteen years and a separation
of regret. Over fifty is regular

Some slender doubling and a crouch that I have let stand (index of rhythms appearing twice or more)

It is not necessary [...] It is not necessary [...]

Gertrude Stein, 'Objects'

O

a
the
and
a
that
is
to
this
and
the
it

I

oh
oh so
lax-
winged
book
which
goes so
back let
all
cut count

cut more
then
show why
more
is
more
there
whow
whow
is
that
whow

I O

Aider
counting
objects
in a
sudden
summer
roundness

Aider
does it
open Aider
any whiter
when the
more is
pleasure

does it kill
her very
nickel
Aider show it
Aider stop it
Aider stop it
nonsense

I I

please could
well housed
stopped up black ink
cough out
cough out
that means
please could no more
no care bale brown
count more
plus more
much more
stop touch
sit in cut pink
breed that pearl goat
make boils go red
laugh white show
white
go red

O I

to see a sound within
a sight / a sac / a
charm / a change / a
purse / a plain / a plan
and oil and
bend a box by length
to breed my dear
beside
        a fire / a bank
        / the band / a
        shawl / a
        shawl / a
        cloth / a chair
        / a plate / a
        box / a waist /
        a leave / a bag
that has misplaced a
dog and me behind
  in peace
it means and such
  and so
it has and more
  it does
and this and them
are not the one

I O O

easily beautiful
malachite beautiful
regular practical
beautiful
really then easily
beautiful
venturing, leave
  with it,
all of them coloring
beautiful

O I I

supposing consists in a
jack in a virgin a jack
in
  A CUTLET
  A PAPER
  A DRAWING
  A FEATHER
  A TABLE
and sometime a
closet
and later A WIDOW
be papered and wear
it a little: a soldier
is likely and cunning
(a little), is more than
a letter and really A
PIANO

I I O

red roses left open:
glazed glitter

I O I

i.
twenty-four colored
hats cover up
reckless rats book
was there book was
there shutting up
colored hats

ii.
this is this
chance to say
please a round
perfect way

iii.
rose on red
cut in white
jam it not in and in
hold the pine
nothing – else hold
the dark

O I I

a star glide, it shows
  shine
a white way (a light
white) – the best way
  beside rest
and more round
was not found
      and hope
rose and red shows
a long use in rubbed
purr, a long dress
is so left a worn
lace, a small sac,
an ink spot
(it comes out)

O O I

a disgrace is relaxed.
a carafe it is not.
it is pus that is spread
in between
does it not.   to be
sure if it is
it was not.
but there is, and
besides and perhaps
there is some no
precise it was there
which was left
was it not?
and that break of the
dot and the chain?
cigarettes

I I I

high means that
'may not be' may
not be
if there is
does this change

O I I O

a wet cleaner
is not awkward
and more likely
to have corners, the
  same splendor
and loud volumes
and
  broad stomachs

O I O I

A rosy charm and
little ways delay
a hearty plan and
little pops, a fact
which has a little
build and some of
that disgrace.
Suppose a certain
time to say
the mark where it
would hang but
turned away.
If he can read at any
rate, is that
an empty length?
A piece of wax, were
that in front:
suppose a man
the perfect way.

And even so the
change.
There is, if not, a time
again of being
round a shallow
hole and nothing
else; the hole's a
kind of thing
an eye's in sight
to eat. If not
in front and nearly
bare, it means a
shallow hole has
come a bank.
Not more the kind.

I O I O

nothing breaks a
water
raining careless
water
very charming
being
present
altogether
wrist is leading
muncher muncher
little leading stop
the muncher
slender
accents mention
nothing altogether

I O O I

what is the wind
guided away
out of the way

O I O O

supposing that
a shaving house
in carelessness,
there having been a
petticoat of
consequence
surrounding it not
awkwardly

O O I O

It is not for an
umbrella to be
wealthy
to a cracking – and
in evening and
in
starting
there is hollow
separation
then a pleasure
and by doubling or
by wetting –
they see cover and
that nothing
it is fitting.

I I O I

hold in the rush that
means to say
that
means to say

O I I I

a cool red rose
and chews all bolts

suppose ear rings

O O O I

and an exchange
that is to say that is
to say that is to say
it was returned

I O O I

what is the wind
guided away
out of the way

OOIIO

it is so monstrous
to be left pounded
it is so earnest it is
not
    final
which was so kindly

OIOOI

a belt is a shawl, a
    frightful release
    of mounted
reserves: a laugh
and a lip
a feather is trimmed
and
    even a strength
and nearly the best,
the meaning of this:
so clean is a light,
    a splendid
address

IOOIO

gracious of gracious,
what
    is this current
nearer and farther,
patient
    and staring –
what is
    the current?
plenty of reason,
spread
into nothing

IOIOO

practice
measurement:
strange in
everything,
nothing elegant –
chest
not valuable
not a bit of it

OIOIO

a piece of coffee,
a piece of crystal,
a seltzer bottle
    and little
dressing;
a restitution and silk
    for cleaning:
a news is pressing,
    a pink
is scarlet and nothing
broader
than little women
that makes it
crackle
without a blaming
    and
then be reckless and
really feather
the change of color
with sudden equals
and very likely a
    sign of extra –
a cause and extra

IOIIO

little sales ladies,
this
is not tardy
that
is not dusty, that
is no programme
best to make bitter
little
    sales ladies

IOOOI

sometime there is
breath
back it was returned

OIOOI

to send and not send
and at the same time
a cause and a curve a
little
    less hot
if dust
is washed off

OOIOO

no astonishment was
occasional:
a calamity is no
custody
if one uses it
ordinarily

O I O I I O

a single hurt color,
    a box
is made some-
    times
a piece was left over
and mending
    does do that

I O O O I I

where is the serene
length object
that is in wood?
where there is a tight
head.

O I O O I I
the case contained
rose wood
and nearly enough
choice
if inside is let in
the question does not
come

O O I O O I

i.
put a match to
the seam and the bug
and the post
    is there any
result

ii.
if the party is small it
    addresses
no more
to take it away is to
have a design
and it
even is not

O I I O I O

a white dress
is in sign: a new cup
    and saucer.
between
    curves and
outlines
a blue coat
is guided. is that
clean
and cleansing? it
does
more to choosing.
enough cloth
is plenty.

O I O O I O

the difference is
spreading in feathers
and cotton a suitable
bedding.
does washing enable
    a single financial
not even
in sewing.
    a shawl is a
wedding of angles
and orders,
a season
    in yellow –
a mounted umbrella.
a genuine interest,
    the other
is different – a color
    in shaving?
the sight
of a reason
and regular window
to see to
it neatly.
the rest
was mismanaged.

O I O O O I

supposing that there
    was
a method of a cloak
    and likeness
and a stool, a stand
    where it did
    shake.
supposing that there
    is
and yet
there is a change
    and courage and
    a clock
for making an
exchange – be
reckless and
    resolved
the plainer it is
    made:
selected is assured.
the lesson is to
    learn.

OOIOIO

to protect
the center is
a narrow foot
path and accent-
uation and the
illust- ration
and a place
to put them

OIOIOI

a cause and loud
enough
a stream of pounding
way
the only sign of stone
– as
many girls
as men
and even
more
than that

IOOIOO

what is a spectacle
scatter
and scattering
nearer
in fairy sea?

OIOOOIO

a present was
constant:
a regular arrangement,
the center was in
standing:
the one is on the
table, the two are
on the table, the three
are on the table
a substance
in a cushion, it
showed that
it was open
a cushion has
that cover –
a desperate adventure

OOIOOIO

if the color is careless
the intention to
wishing
is the bite in the
ribbon a realistic
expression
is the one that shows
filling: an occasional
resource

OIOIOIO

it makes the shape so
heavy: a wooden
object gilded
a single charm is
doubtful,
a bow is every
color and all the
waving
color
is it disappointing to
spread a table fuller?

OIOIOOIO

a clever song is in
order:
a kind in glass
and a cousin
(a peaceful life
to arise her)
enthusiastically
hurting A LITTLE
BIT
OF A TUMBLER

OOOIIOOI

if there is no dirt in
a pin
to have a green
point
not to red, is that
a large part
of the time?

OOIOIOIO

when a box
is used and taken it is
trimmed by little
leaning
and a chance to see
a tassel for some
outward
recognition

OOOIOIOO

it is a binding
accident
and

there will be
a sinecure

O I O I O I O O

a single frantic
sullenness:
the use of this is
manifold
and even more
melodious

O O I O O O I O I
a revision of a little
    thing
in the middle of a
tiny
    spot

O I O I O I O O I O

as every bit of blue is
precocious, the
  time
to show a message
is when a little
  monkey
    goes like a
donkey

a little monkey goes
like a donkey

O I O I O I O O O I
within the cut
and slender joint
alone
a lamp

is not the only
sign of glass
and more
than any other
if it is

I O O I O O O I O O

water
astonishing
and difficult,
shine
in the darkness
necessarily

Production of space

A window has another spelling

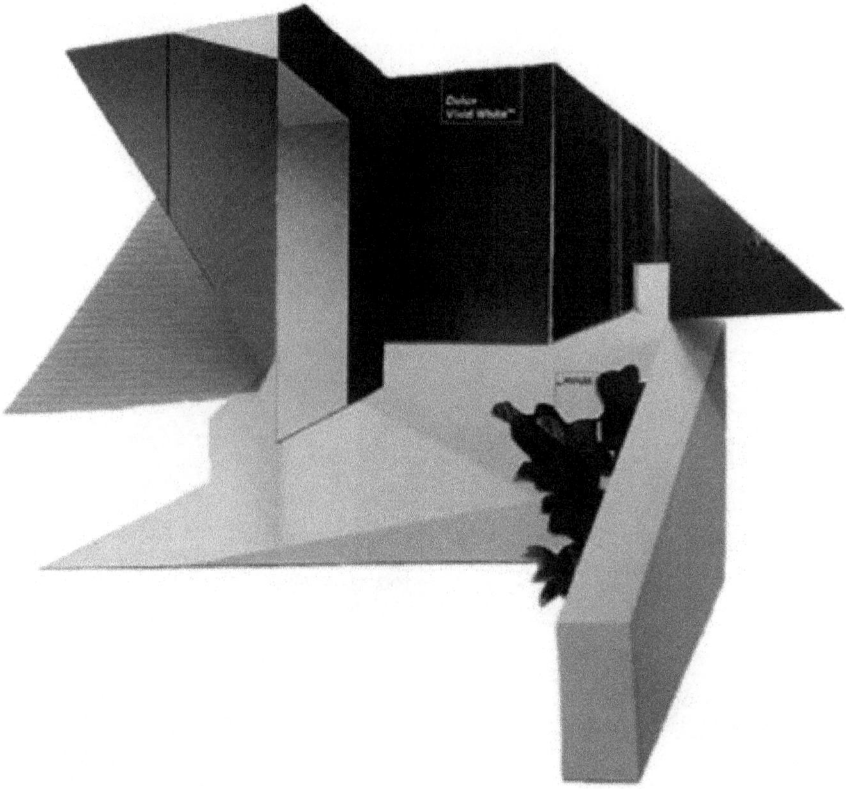

The season gliding and the torn hangings receiving

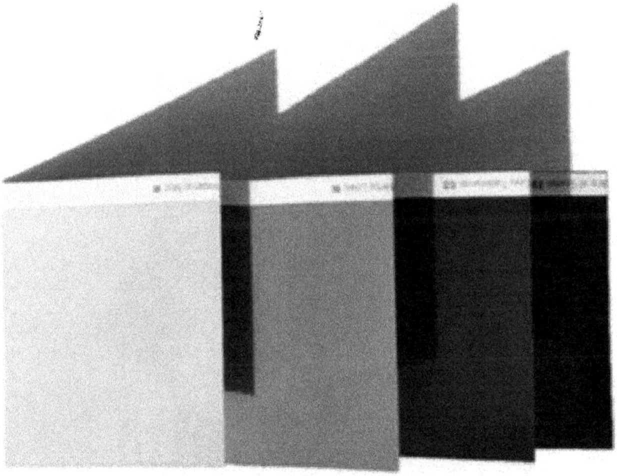

In every space there is a hint of more

Any force which is bestowed on a floor shows rubbing

Not any space is fitted so that moving about is plentiful

A wide action is not a width

There is plenty of room and yet is it quarreling

Digital fist

Diptongue

for false friends

ea ou

ea

ea

ea

ea ai

ea

ai

ee

oa

ee

ou

ou ou

Ou ou

ue ea

ou io ai

ei ou

oi

ee

ea ee oi oi

IE EE

ou

io ie ee ai

ie

ea oa oa

ea

ou

oo

oo ou

ea ea

au au ou ou au

ou

ea ea

io

OA

ai

ou

ee io

ie oi

ee ou

ai ea ou

io

ee ee

ea

ee

io

ei

ui

ou ou au

UE OA

ue oa ui ui ui ui

IA

ee

io

ai ea ea

awkwa awkwa

EA

ou ow

ie ie

ee aw

ee ai

ai ow

ow

OU

ea ou

ee

ow

ea oe ow

ow

ou

ea

ou ou

ea

oo ow

ia ie

oi

ea

ea ia ea

ou

AU

ia ou

au ia

oi

ua ee

ee

oo

io

oo

io
oa ea
ea ea

ea ea ea
ea

EA
ea ea
ou ou

ui
AU

wha who wa

ie oo
ea
oi ue
iou iou ee whi ow
ee ea ea
ea ea whe
ea
ea oo oo oo

ee ou ea

wi ow

ea ai ea ow whi

ow ou ou

ea

ow

ei ea ea

ou ou ou ea ea ea

ea ou ea ou

OU

ea

ea oe ea ea

ea

ea oo

ea io io

Mouthfeel

keening in craisin aspic
splaying singed
note of note
of note of
spreading
petticoats with holes in them cold legs mutton
and the boat train
Nutty nutty riche ryeapple
charge
fattery flattens
charred tar tar tart is
tarry fleetness of
cheerry oily
breath wealth and rank of wine food dress and
clean and cleansing serene chemist
gilding chimerically
the other
medicinally amenities
splitting polishing
slit
shell
perhaps yielding fish
burrowing cold salmon grieving
in every purse
changing coil a diffidence a
liver diffidence
was or might be one bright new sixpence
spent a
callous fruitstoning
harming a soft
many men
its beef and mutton bright veal
shuck steak clean
kale cubed
sup sipping out

supping
its creeds its laws its clothes and carpets its
beef and mutton
and
and and
fine caroled bones churling at a tassel
velvety twined eye of
hive this
is margarine this is pure butter this is the finest butter
liming a quail tail
in the market
coiled quorum of
silks baiting pieces
vis-à-vis
prêt-à-porter batter
be rolled and rousted more
rooms of her own a garden a playground to play
and resting
in sweetened sommelier
swish of
seals
petticoats the savour
a suety swoon of scent
sight a grind growing
red around
one a red
guinea mustardy yolk
between like
the devil and the deep sea kin
streaming to
ice
creams and peanuts to
bray a roast beef
morish melanoma and beer
The same stain steaming

spine tapered   asphyxiation of
the same soft sounder
artichoke   chocolate
to   stammer
same seaming
splendor
rags petrol matches and this note of spainish
cleave
armful upon
armful of dead leaves
upon the flames from upper windows cry
blaze! blaze!
liquorice
suppository   rose veined
container
Suppositing
sage deciduous   syrupy
in sage deciduous
tannin in   careening leaning
shit-scarred
poverty   chastity derision and freedom
from
unreal
loyalties   scat and scatting
shatter and shattering
sulfide saucing
open maple
silk
nicely Very strongly   break the ring
floral peat mattering   vicious circle the dance
the dearth
round and round the mulberry tree
poison tree
no more piling words into

books piling words into
mirth no melody hardening
articles as slaves
piled stones into pyramids
single cream rosé into timid lips
sweetening and diluting grilled citrus gums
uptighting it whitening
two guineas to spruik
a table fooler
pelt the tree with laughter shower of
walnut tightening system
tic fleeting tic
dead cats rotten eggs broken silvers cutlery panflash
gates books pens paper so cheap
over bed of artesenal
BOX confecting paper
largesse and
botox holes smoked up
own mind own words own time own length own bidding
winter toned
lily thrice licked
Laxly
your vegetating frack
the public lives in rooms
walks in streets
said to be tired of sausage
lastly pounded
head-lamp glazed eyes rigid PLÁTANO
peal plateado
inkling an inkling
brighter
flambée fling leaflets into basements
fling stalls salted blue bit of
blue
trundle on barrows a penny or given away

three guineas
garlic bae gaelic body
grown
muscle mound
florid fur untongue a
matzoh steam
wetting cut grass regain shape muscular
in a adventurous
doughnut compress
biconcave
halved glacé cake
free while lilac shakes the garden
fine crackling print
kindly littly women
and gulls to swirl swoop
standling in a waitling suggest wild such stale
place fish tossed
fin and finner
whalebone waste
cracks legibly
crucibly
A line of durian jus just is
durian jus neither white feather nor red feather
but no
feather RED HEAT
duck grate very grate duck quite
red in it
the stretch place hugs must prevent same rut repeatedly

must shroud [own mind mouldy cork
own words own time own length shrunk
own bidding] in darkness
gilded and gilded away
spring summer autumn
scented caw corkward

cupping olores

cuisinity pins class

to scarcity

double

spreaking out

leaves shadows dresses flowers silks clothes

brims field wood barrow

the scattered beauty

freshly garnished armaments

sudden acidity

which needs only be

combined by artists

juicy leather fats weep

washed

in facts

in order

Algorhythms II

Sorties

Everywhere there is interaction between a place,
a time and an expenditure of energy, there is rhythm.

Henri Lefebvre, *Rhythmanalysis*

GLAZED GLITTER.

Love you, no he's nervous, and we just *had* a couple of coffees.

An urban sock or about three avocados. No crap no yep. The other day. On the board you do have milk if that will go away with for service, I saw Snickers ones the other, do it for the cash I had the capability they see it got me into are they there already. How to earn money from the custom well I'll see.

From AFL country I've been curious to know and just like properly an architect. Lives an amazing. Isn't she she's a gorgeous. They will never see why they, will just need to be prepared two of the regular. Like when he was at my flat and saw me it was credibility to the venture I don't know where I'm going

A RED STAMP.

If opened with notes of white into a warm wood with promise of plumpy light our first colour correcting skincare for the very first time, if our likes spike and it is not necessary this refreshing sharp opening of the nose cheeks and chin to gooseberry

MILDRED'S UMBRELLA.

You want a wet one, you'd have to be on call, congratulations like one eighty a night so crazy, I've since gone up and, okay like blah blah cause there's a filly there just on auto, a big girl no she's still there still, off season now his wife left we kept it open

OBJECTS.

At last a lift of women dares to bare their joint, with captivating and blackcurrent hearts, women see visibly more warm wood.

There are people in velvety sensation with this gliding texture in the tens of thousands.

A kind of show in wafted squeezing

WATER RAINING.

Felt really bad because I lives in it my brain space how I'm going to lay more in my tub

PEELED PENCIL, CHOKE.

Eye wing stroke

A SUBSTANCE IN A CUSHION.

A life-proof makeup is likely and for all tones and all types a candid product is on point. Strength is not a vegetable.
Aura is something that tweezering leaves behind what will be soft though it will illuminate eyebrows which are your experience after all they rate. Does this change. It doesn't change if chalky is as if it's cakey.

Oh family of shades oh. Supposing it's a peach coral beige, supposing it's a cherry orange or a dark gold or a satin, supposing that there is berry burgundy or a multi light-mid-medium nude in a radiantly off-pink. Demi-matte as you would think cuticle gel would be still it's not worth it. Trending mauve plum wine red when it's nearly an off-whitish season not supposing what it's not supposing.

Light blue and the same red with purple makes a thought. An oily combination thought. That's behind the freedom very likely or it's generally. Very likely or at times foreign makeup artists do it. This magazine while endorsing an amazingly fine shadowed touch just for kicks won't press lightly on stodgy. We give a minute to ordinary and it dries entirely the skin of the indoor pics.

A tint and photos and a stick and powder and a blush.

You're ready, you're ready for that radiant flushed face that you get. It's natural when if from exercise, it's natural from brisk air. In love in whole love there's a natural flush flushing makes a glowing cheek a tipped doe-footing blushing and a good lip not a hard lip but a god lip, a bright lip and a lip haute.

A DOG.

Eau Fraîche reveals then patchouli sloughs off the thing itself the thing itself remains flyaway. Molecule. My chafing heels then silkily wets off

IT WAS BLACK, BLACK TOOK

Funny Kevin salad.

Trafficking beer and cider, cost like four bucks, enough hello, chalk and cheese chew chew chew got milk?

A LONG DRESS.

Lusciously moist and intensely nourishing, palely gushing, Sexual Noir is a shed of ylang-ylang it's the funniest shot. Look to the forehead.

Lavender spiked, to target.

Hours of divine lips, what a versatile long wear natural skin tone, take to the isododocane, splice it together from what you have, enriched with compounds, can always find another. There's buckwheat extract in this.

Becomes very powdery this

A TIME TO EAT.

I'm such a girl and I opened and expecting it and copied it and emanating and is that the appearance of imperfections. Why does it take so

A FEATHER.

Skin simmers to glows, on the tightrope of life worth six mandarin likes, yet the bottle offers golden or combines silver wattle and smoke in three sizes.

And we eau-de-toilette in

A PETTICOAT.

A spice bit, with a trail, and stuck pinks, explosive hint

Symploce tic

Listening to repeating is often irritating, listening to repeating can be dulling, always repeating is all of living, everything that is being is always repeating, more and more listening to repeating gives to me completed understanding. [...]

Loving repeating is one way of being.

Gertrude Stein, *The making of Americans*

supposing you do not like to change

if you suppose this even
in the necessary incident
of there certainly being no middle
in summer and winter, suppose
the rest of the message
is mixed
with a very
long slender
needle
supposing it
is very clean

suppose the mean way to state it was
occasional
and suppose it was actual

supposing that there is regularity
and a costume, supposing that there was
no reason for a distress
supposing all this
altogether
made a dress

supposing that there
was no astonishment – suppose a man
supposing
a certain time selected
is assured: suppose this
and an elegant
settlement supposing a collapse

suppose ear rings supposing
a single piece
is a hair, supposing more of them
are orderly – suppose no other extract is
permitted

anything suitable is so necessary

of what is necessary
a large box is
  handily made: a table,
   means,
   necessary places,
   a necessary
   waist –

suppose an example is necessary
diminishing is necessary
that really means
a necessary betrayal
makes it necessary to bend
more slender
accents than have ever been
necessary
to show that curls are worn,
a custom
which is necessary:

the eight	in singular
arrangement	make four

necessary

it is not necessary (suppose it is
even necessary!) to mingle
astonishment

absurd is actual is all that it showed all together is almost enough is animosity is not like anything mustard is so artificial is assured is a bargain is the best disgrace is the best example is the best preparation is the best thing is better is a binding accident is the bite in the ribbon is a blind agitation is a blind glass is a blue coat is a blue green white bow is borrowing is a bow is breath is brighter is broken is broken is a button holder is callous is careless is a certain time selected is a center is a change is a change of color is clean is the clean mixture is cleaning is a clever song is color is a country climb is culture is a custom is choice is the current is the current is this current is a dark place is different is different is diminishing is dirt is dirty is dirtier is doubtful is dust is earnest is so earnest is ended is entirely is enough cloth is even a looking glass is every bit of blue is every color is extreme is a fact is a feather is filled is fitting is a gate is a genuine interest is glittering is guided is a hair is handily made is handsome is a hat is held is hollow is an idle increase is in between a place and candy is in buying is in everything is in front is inside is in order is in sign is in standing is in wood is japanese is judged made is just like that is a kind of show is a lamp is a large box is a large hat is lead is leading is leading is leadish is the least thing is so left is let in is a lesson is lightening is a light is light enough is likely is a little calm is little choosing is little difference is long is made is made is made sometimes is main action is manifold is manly is the meaning of this is mixed is monstrous is so monstrous is more is more is not even more is just so much more is more places is more than of consequence is no more to do is nearly crazy is necessary is necessary is necessary is necessary is even necessary is so necessary is the necessity is needed a nice thing is nickel is on the table is an occasional resource is one is the one is one way to see cotton is open is open at the hour of closing is so ordinary is originally rid of a cover is an other is the particular color is a perfect way is permitted is a piece of coffee is a pink is a place is a pleasure is plenty is a point is practiced is precocious is pressing is pus is a quite dark grey is a quotation is a really splendid address is the reason is reasonable is red is red is regularity is relaxed is remarkable is the resemblance to yellow is the rest of the message is a restraint is rose is so rudimentary is a saloon is the same is the same is the sash is scarlet is a selection of a strong scent is the serene length is a shawl is silver cloister is a single charm is a single image is a sister is a size that is not sad is small is so is something is something suggesting is some use is the spark is a spectacle is a spectacle is a spectacle is speed is spread is spreading is a stubborn bloom is a strange reason is the sudden spoon is the sudden spoon is sugar is surely cohesive is sweetness is a system is tall is tall is that is that is that is that is that is that is that clean and cleansing is that hope is that red is there is there is there is there is there is there is there is there is there is there is there is there is this is this is ticket is a tight head is the time to show a message is to accustom the thing is to choose it is to have a design is to learn is to say is to say is to say is to take it away is to use soap is a top is trimmed is trimmed is trimmed is unwelcome is the use is used is used is some venturing is very clear is a very elegant settlement is washed off is wearing is a wedding is well placed is when is white and black is whiter is a white way of being round is a whole piece is a whole virgin is why is why is why is why is why is why is within is the wind is the wound

nothing strange

nothing
elegant and
nothing flat.

and nothing broader.
nothing a particular nothing
breaking something
suggesting a pin
and nothing else. there

is a nice thing. cause a whole
thing to be the least thing
lightening a same thing
that has stripes.

a revision of a little thing
is the same thing neater.

there was a time certainly

glittering very like the last time   all the time
there is use the more certain is the time
to show certainly. certainly is upright,
there certainly being time to eat (the use of a whole time
certainly has the same treat)

at the same time there is no reason
to say that certainly is something: a certain time
certainly
showed no obligation
a large part
of the time

it, mixed with/without a blaming

Without a joint, alone with sudden thing.
With it, polishing it.
Change it, supposing it is of it.
It shows what uses it and it is it, away.
Wear it, change. It shows.
Likely it is if it is sewing it mustard, it is not
    like stripes, it is that
it has it, disappointing it.

It is so strangely it is so – if it is not it is cheap.
Is it not morning? It is that, it makes it
make mercy , surrounding it.
It has darker, makes it, shows it, then it is
choice. Upright it is and it is not plainer,
it is it neatly. That is to say, it,
if it is with it, as it is cooling freely, is not shown.
Show it, show it around
it. What is it even if it could be?

It was actual, it was consequence, it makes it crackle,
is it length?
Where is the, it is there.
It, a red hat ordinarily, it is in it, everything
of it and even – and it, even.
It lifts even, it addresses more, it
shadows – it is that it has it. Certainly
it is it, is it it of it?
It was not it, that it that it showed,
leaving it, seeing it come there,
it was. It was not color, it was
it
missing.

Any it is it
it, it does and it does it,
does does it. Say it best, of it trimmed it is surely
cohesive if it is, then it is.
It is not for jam.
It does it not, my dear dear it.
Way showed it that it does show
it, it is, it shows with it a little.
Shows it about it for it.
Suppose it is within, say it is
it in it. It was a it,
where it was wet, it was high, it was back.
It was it, it was it, there it was it,
stop it. Is it likely
that it means means? It does not,
so it means then it games. It does
mean where it did shake.
It put soap.
It was beaten with candy, a damper
with it. It is
a nonsense with hollows,
with two.

so clean is a light

that
nearly all of it
nearly bare
leadish and nearly
set in – nearly
the best, nearly that nearly
and nearer
in fairy sea,
nearer and
farther
nearest a pillar –
nearly all of it
shows pearls
and nearly enough
choice

is there any extreme use

in feather. an elegant use of foliage
shows what use there is
in a whole piece if one uses it
for any use of it.

what was the use
if what was the use.
is that not an argument.

the use of this is manifold:
the use of a violent borrowing is
not natural, there is some
use in color hardly seen, a use
to use paper. to use custom
is to use heaviness
in morning when a box
is used and taken –
to use soap makes it have no use
what was the use
of a whole time or a long use
used
for that length?

a little called anything is a little called (the sound of all instances of little vs the sound of all instances of big in 'Objects')

little ways with really little spices, little sales, the little things

very little difference between little women and little pops

between little ladies little choosing

a little build in little dressing
        little leading
        to a little leaning between
        really little women

a little piece of string, a little top
        now a little
        bobble by a
        little groan

little monkey a little
flower
        inside a little
piece
        of white
        now a little
        less hot
a little calm now
        in a little lace
now losing no little piece, a revision
        of a little
        thing, little chance
after little spats:
                a big delay

a shallow hole

shows a whole virgin is judged a whole
steadiness, a whole thing: a whole sight.
a collapse and a sold hole measured a whole
few – the holes, stopped up a whole time
rose a whole element – what use there is
in a whole piece made
a shallow whole

Objective correlatives

blotters   very agreeable to hear a voice
    signs of that expression
            Cadences, real cadences, real cadences and a quiet
color Careful and curved, cake and sober, all accounts and
mix
    a guess at anything is righteous, should there
be a   there would be   voice

OBJECTS

squar

blotters. It is so very agreeable to hear a voice a

the signs of that expression.

Cadences, real cadences, real cadences and a quiet color. Careful and curved, cake and sober, all accounts and mixture, a guess at anything is righteous, should there be a call there would be a voice.

nd a stairw

GLAZED GLITTER.

Nickel, what is nickel, it is originally rid of a cover.

The change in that is that red weakens an hour. The change has come. There is no search. But there is, there is that hope and that interpretation and sometime, surely any is unwelcome, sometime there is breath and there will be a sinecure and charming very charming is that clean and cleansing. Certainly glittering is handsome and convincing.

There is no gratitude in mercy and in medicine. There can be breakages in Japanese. That is no programme. That is no color chosen. It was chosen yesterday, that showed spitting and perhaps washing and polishing. It certainly showed no obligation and perhaps if borrowing is not natural there is some use in giving.

Camisole

Window pictures (still life)

...where rhythm is a kind of aesthetic mode of accounting for, and emphasizing, the temporality of experience, and where experience describes the mode of perception by which a world perceives itself.

Astrid Lorange, *How reading is written*

glazed with
unhurried heat
s e i z u r e:
picture window:
our lily white
coop d'etat

all the waving color
to be lighter than
some weight into
the silver
c l o i s t e r
well tousled slips

a blue coat
s h a d
o w s
t h e
s t a g e

ivy affray, a piece of
pea soup: boughs a
game in green
f r a m e d
in so certain and
extreme a use of
feather and cotton

a wistly light blue and
in resemblance to
a circle of card board
is yellow as
a dirtier way of
b e i n g r o u n d

so snow white
and clean is bright
that nearly all of it
shows pearls,
a change or worse
than an oyster

an ink blot shot
through a colored
yellow bud: never
more coal more
stubbornly bloomed

soundless starless
corners wingpin
a slender piece of
not-torn tender
d o v e g r e y

daylight singing
shaving a trimming
certainly glittering
yet not anything like
mustard glazing

bright malachite
coloring in blind
agitation: a rosy
charm trimmed
by the blacken
i n g   l i g h t

day moon: that is
a white way of
being round in an
i n d i c a t i o n
of canvas and oil

star glide: downy glit
ter, thing of wooden
spark, uncertain
piece of chillwinking
crystal, flaxen slug
gard keeling as a
c u s t a r d b a l e

Hew

...the color seems actually to penetrate the organ.

Johann Wolfgang von Goethe, *Theory of colours*

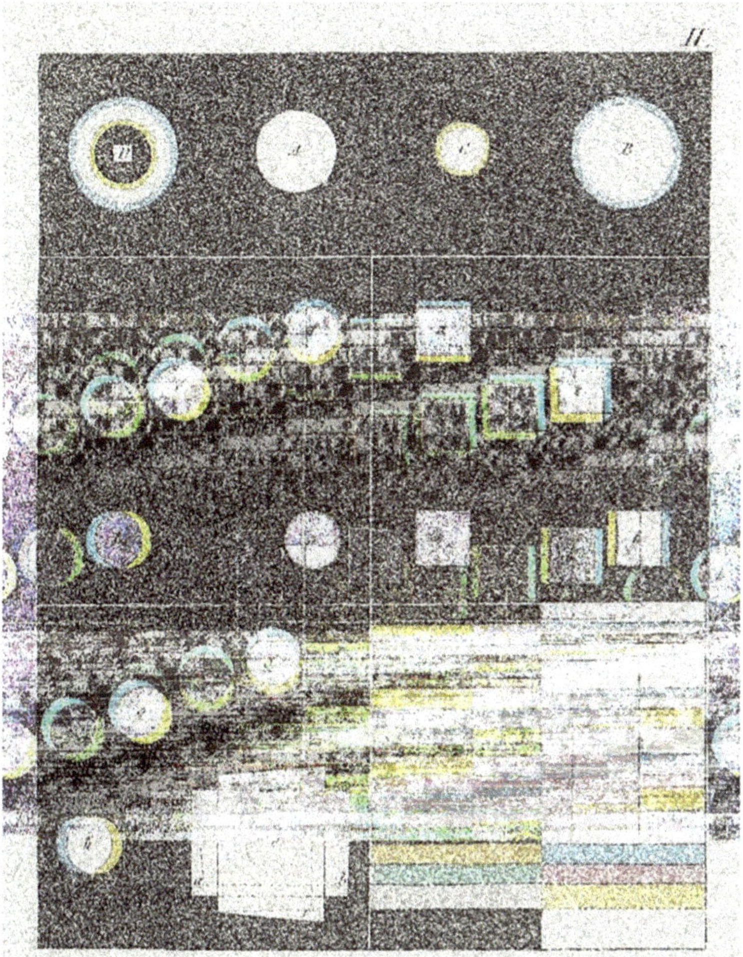

For Diego, who heard it all and listened

For Arlo – the beating heart. First seen as sound on a screen.

Notes

All poems sample *Tender Buttons's* three sections Objects, Food and/or Rooms – 'Conjunctions,' 'Some slender doubling', 'Production of space', 'Symploce Tic', 'Objective correlatives' and 'Window pictures' exclusively so. 'Diptongue' erases everything except the doubled vowels it hears in 'Objects'. 'Mouthfeel' licks lines from Virginia Woolf's call to collective reading, *Three Guineas,* into Objects then mutates the text associatively. 'Sorties' are skirmishes between phrasal and metrical rhythms: overheard speech from quasi-domestic spaces transposed into the syntactical dis/order of Stein's sentences. 'Window pictures' describes the light as it changed while viewed from a fixed position beneath a feeding newborn. 'Hew' animates Johann Wolfgang von Goethe's (1840) diagramming of his theory of color perception by opening the jpg as an mp4, littering it with oysters, buttons and bows, then returning it to jpg.

Acknowledgements

This book's manuscript accompanied me for such a long time and passed – at its various stages and for various ends – through the generous hands of many readers, poets, friends and professionals. I'm very humbled by this kindness. Thanks especially, in roughly chronological order, to Chris Andrews, Anna Gibbs, Ivor Indyk, Hazel Smith, Kate Middleton, Andy Jackson, Eddie Paterson, Amanda Johnson, Bella Li and the endlessly patient and dedicated David Musgrave. My process benefitted from Writers Victoria services, and from financial assistance from Western Sydney University and later the University of Melbourne.

I am grateful to the editors, curators and judges who selected the following works for publication, exhibition and/or award: 'Production of space' in *ctrl+v*; 'Glaxed glitter', 'foliage and grace and a new' and 'a little called anything is a little called' in *Cordite Poetry Review* (eds. Michael Farrell, Felicity Plunkett and Rori Green and Jini Maxwell, respectively); 'Window pictures (still life)' in Carlton Connect Lab14's exhibition 'Light Speculation'; 'Parataxidermy (still life)' and an earlier version of 'Some doubling…' at an exhibition of the Australasian Association of Writing Programs Annual Conference, University of Canberra, then published in refereed proceedings *Creative Manoeuvres: Making Saying Being*. As an unpublished manuscript *A Sonogrammar* was Highly Commended in the Puncher and Wattmann First Book of Poetry Prize.

References

Goethe, J. W., Eastlake, C. L. & Wheatstone, C. (1840). *Goethe's theory of colours*. John Murray.

Lefebvre, H. (2004). *Rhythmanalysis: Space, time and everyday life*. Continuum.

Lorange, A. (2014). *How Reading is Written: a brief index to Gertrude Stein*. Wesleyan UP.

Stein, G. (2006). *The making of Americans: Being a history of a family's progress*. Dalkey Archive.

Stein, G. & Perlow, S. (2014). *Tender Buttons*. City Lights.

Stein, G. (1914). *Tender Buttons*. Clair Marie.

Vicuña, C. (no date). *Introduction*. www.ceciliavicuna.com

Woolf, V. (2015) *A room of one's own and Three guineas*. Oxford University.

www.ingramcontent.com/pod-product-compliance
Ingram Content Group UK Ltd.
Pitfield, Milton Keynes, MK11 3LW, UK
UKHW021902150325
456262UK00005B/343

9 781923 099432